BIBLICAL ECONOMICS

STUDY GUIDE

DR. R.C. SPROUL JR.

"Where there is no vision, the people perish."

The Vision Forum, Inc.
4719 Blanco Rd., San Antonio, Texas 78212
1-800-440-0022
www.visionforum.com
ISBN-10 1-934554-48-0
ISBN-13 978-1-934554-48-7

Cover Design and Typography by Justin Turley

Printed in the United States of America

OTHER BOOKS *from* VISION FORUM

Table of Contents

Introduction

According to Genesis, before God gave the command to worship, before He gave the command to not eat of the Tree of the Knowledge of Good and Evil, He commanded Adam and Eve to work, to be fruitful and multiply, to fill the earth and subdue it, and to rule over the living creatures. Of course worship is critically important. Obedience is critically important as well. But so too is our labor. Too many of us take a Gnostic approach to work. We see it, at best, as a necessary evil, something we do to keep body and soul together so we can be about the really important stuff—our souls. God, however, called His creation good. Our Lord Jesus took on flesh and did so not just to save our souls, but to save us to the uttermost—to save our souls and our bodies which will be raised again in glory on that great and final day. Until that time, we have work to do.

This is why we are so pleased that you have chosen to study some basic biblical principles of economics with us. The study you are about to embark on isn't in the end about arcane numerical formulae. It isn't about dusty ledgers or computer models. You will not come away equipped to trade in the futures markets. It is instead about the most basic questions we all face. It is about how our loving Father answers our prayer, "Give us this day our daily bread" (Matthew 6:11). It is likely as you progress through this study, as you come to understand the folly of our economic disobedience, that you will from time to time become disheartened, perhaps even afraid. Those are the times that we must return to first principles. None is more basic than this, "In the beginning, God created the heavens and the earth" (Genesis 1:1).

Our study of economics is a study of our stewardship of God's creation. We must remember always that He not only owns the cattle on a thousand hills, but all the cattle on all the hills, all the hills, the grass on those hills, the rain that waters the grass, and the sun that makes it grow. It is all His, just as we are His. Our prayer then is that this study will equip you to be a more faithful and wise steward, and that, while all those around you are in panic, you will rest in the sovereign reign of Jesus over all things.

Ideas have consequences. Foolish ideas have dangerous consequences. But no matter how foolish we might be, no matter how badly politicians might gum up the economy, they cannot wrest God from His heavenly throne.

May God bless you richly as you embark on this study of biblical economics. And may He be pleased to prosper you and your labors. May He give you peace and use you to bring all things under subjection for the glory of His Son, our Lord.

Dr. R.C. Sproul Jr.
September 2010
Orlando, Florida

Study Course Syllabus
A Note to Parents

There was a time when most every citizen had at least a rudimentary understanding of economics. We are not in that time. You have chosen this curriculum in all likelihood because of the confluence of two things. First, you believe your child or children need such an understanding. Second, you believe you are not in a position to give them that understanding.

Our desire in creating this curriculum is not just that your child would come to understand these things, but that you would as well. If you are persuaded, as we hope you are, that your child needs to understand economics, you ought to recognize that you need to understand it too. This curriculum certainly could be used by your child alone. For it to be most effective, however, it ought to be used by you and your child together. In the end, the principles of biblical economics are not at all complicated. Much of what we will be doing is clearing away the cobwebs of political machinations. You can learn these things, and so can your child.

The program is designed this way. Students, and we pray parents, should read the assigned reading prior to listening to the lecture. Afterwards, parent and student should discuss what was learned with the aid of the discussion questions provided. (Of course you are encouraged to come up with your own questions.)

There are twelve lectures, thus twelve sections. Each section, we are confident, could be accomplished in a week without overwhelming other studies. They could be done more quickly, or they could be done more slowly. That is up to you. After the third section, there is a brief quiz, along with an answer key. Again, parents are encouraged not only to correct the quiz, but to take it. There is a similar quiz after the ninth section.

After the sixth section, there is a mid-term exam. This (like everything else in this curriculum) is optional. Some of you may instead wish to assign instead a research paper. Here are some suggestions for themes that could be addressed:

- Write a biographical paper on a well-known and influential economist. (Adam Smith, Thomas Malthus, John Maynard Keynes, Ludwig Von Mises, Murray Rothbard, Milton Friedman, Walter Williams, and Thomas Sowell are some suggestions);

- Write a paper on the history of the Federal Reserve banking system in these United States;

- Write a paper on the history of gold as a medium of exchange;

- Write a paper doing a word study on a key biblical term, like money, or work, or even laziness;

- Write a paper on the story of Naboth's vineyard and the history of imminent domain;

At the end of the twelve sections, there is also a final exam. If you as the parent are studying with the student, you should be in a position to give grades, if you so wish, to the exam(s) and/or paper. If you do not wish to do so, Highlands Ministries will, for a modest fee, grade the exam(s) and/or paper. Simply contact us at info@highlandsministriesonline.org for instructions on doing this.

Here is how we have designed the course to be implemented, section by section:

Section I — Read Genesis 1-3 prior to lecture. Listen to Lecture 1 and discuss.

Section II — Read *Biblical Economics* Foreword through Chapter 2. Listen to Lecture 2 and discuss.

Section III — Read *Biblical Economics* Chapter 3 through Chapter 4. Listen to Lecture 3 and discuss.

Section IV — Read *Biblical Economics* Chapter 5. Listen to Lecture 4 and discuss.

Section V — Read *Biblical Economics* Chapter 6 through Chapter 8. Listen to Lecture 5 and discuss.

Section VI — Prepare for mid-term exam, or begin work on research paper. Listen to Lecture 6 and discuss. Take exam if choosing that option.

Section VII — Read *Biblical Economics* Chapter 9 through Chapter 10. Listen to Lecture 7 and discuss.

Section VIII — Read *Biblical Economics* Chapter 11 to the end. Listen to Lecture 8 and discuss.

Section IX — Read *The Law* by Frederic Bastiat. Listen to Lecture 9 and discuss. Take second quiz.

Section X — Read the first third of *Productive Christians in an Age of Guilt Manipulators* by David Chilton. Listen to Lecture 10 and discuss.

Section XI — Read the second third of *Productive Christians*. Listen to Lecture 11 and discuss.

Section XII — Finish *Productive Christians*. Listen to Lecture 12 and discuss. Take final exam. Paper, if that option is taken, is due.

Lesson 1
Creation

Summary

The Bible begins with this pregnant, fruitful sentence: "In the beginning God created the heavens and the earth." Our study of economics begins in the exact same place. Economics is the study of our rule over the creation as God's stewards, of how we reflect His image in re-creating, even as He is the Creator, and even how our own sovereignty over what is ours reflects His sovereignty over all things.

God not only created the world, but the Bible tells us, "God saw that it was good" (Genesis 1:25). This, of course, reminds us that the material world isn't somehow icky or unspiritual. It tells us, in fact, that if we would be spiritual, we must be not just concerned with the created order, but in ruling over it. We pray that you will come away from this first lesson well established in the first principle: that God made and owns everything.

Discussion Questions

1. What other fields of study besides economics might we expect to find wisdom for in the Bible?

_____

_____

_____

_____

2. How does the creation account in Genesis inform our beginning principles of understanding economics?

_____

_____

_____

_____

3. How does our understanding that God created the world out of nothing impact our understanding of economics?

_____

_____

_____

_____

4. How are we best able to discern the principles by which God designed the world? What can we learn from the order of the universe about God? What is the message declared by the heavens in Psalm 19?

_____

_____

_____

_____

_____

5. How might an evolutionary view of the beginning of the world impact how we look at economic issues?

_____

_____

_____

_____

_____

6. Is God's grace evident in creation, even before the fall of mankind?

_____

_____

_____

_____

_____

Memory Verses

Genesis 1:1, "In the beginning God created the heavens and the earth."

Psalm 24:1, "The earth is the Lord's and all its fullness, the world and those who dwell therein."

Lesson 2
Stewardship

Summary

Karl Marx once spoke wisdom when he described man as *homo faber*—man, the maker. Work isn't just something we do in order to live the rest of our lives. It instead is part and parcel of what and who we are. It is central to our bearing the very image of God. Work, we would be wise to remember, was a gift from God to our first parents, even while they were yet still in Eden's paradise. The Fall did not create labor, but brought a curse upon it.

When we work for ourselves, we show ourselves the enemies of God. When, however, we work as His stewards, we live in the context of blessing. We will still struggle with thorns and thistles, but our work will bring honor and glory of our God, and therefore will lead Him to say to us, "Well done, [thou] good and faithful servant" (Matthew 25:23).

Discussion Questions

1. Before the Fall, what was man's place in the order of creation? What was man called to be and to do?

_____

_____

_____

_____

_____

2. Where did our labor fit into the calling that God placed on us in the Garden?

_____

_____

_____

_____

_____

3. What ought to be the end goal of all of our labors?

_____

_____

_____

_____

_____

4. How did the Fall of man in Adam impact our experience of labor?

_____

_____

_____

_____

_____

_____

5. How does the work of those outside the kingdom of God relate to our calling under God as humans?

_____

_____

_____

_____

6. Has the dominion mandate—the call to fill the earth and subdue it, to be fruitful and multiply—been abolished?

_____

_____

_____

_____

Memory Verses

Genesis 1:26, "Then God said, 'Let us make man in Our image, according to Our likeness; let them have dominion over the fish of the sea, over the birds of the air, and over the cattle, over all the earth and over every creeping thing that creeps on the earth.'"

Genesis 3:19, "In the sweat of your face you shall eat bread till you return to the ground, for out of it you were taken; for dust you are and to dust you shall return."

Lesson 3
Prosperity

Summary

God has not hidden from us the path to prosperity. Indeed the path is clearly marked. We prosper when we consume less than we produce, even as we face poverty when we consume more than we produce. There are in turn two critical tools to bring this to pass. First, we produce more through the right use of tools. Tools are the very engines of our productivity. The better the tools, the more we are able to produce.

Second, we must learn to delay gratification. We must learn to be content in what God has in His grace provided. We must learn gratitude. We find ourselves, as families and as nations, in economic trouble not ultimately because we do not understand economics, but because we are sinners. One wise pundit encourages us to live like no one else (that is, frugally) so that we might later live like no one else (that is, enjoy prosperity). One still wiser told us that the first would be last, and the last first.

Discussion Questions

1. What is the First Law of Economics? Why is it so easy to forget this?

_____

_____

_____

_____

_____

2. What is the First Law of Prosperity? Why is it so easy to forget this?

_____

_____

_____

_____

_____

3. What does consuming less than we produce allow us to do?

_____

_____

_____

_____

_____

4. Why are tools so critical to the success of our pursuit of material welfare?

_____

_____

_____

_____

5. What is the key character quality necessary to helping us consume less than we produce?

_____

_____

_____

_____

_____

6. How does the Tenth Commandment fit in with that character quality?

_____

_____

_____

_____

_____

Memory Verses

Psalm 50:10, "For every beast of the forest is Mine, and the cattle on a thousand hills."

Proverbs 14:4, "Where no oxen are, the trough is clean; but much increase comes by the strength of an ox."

Lesson 4
Profit

Summary

Liberty alone is the environment or context wherein widespread prosperity can prevail. A free economy is a blessed economy. An economy under the thumb of the state is a stagnant economy. This is not simply because God blesses liberty and punishes tyranny directly, but because of simple economic laws. Tinkering with the very design of God never helps things turn out well.

In this lesson, we will learn of the power and wisdom of an oft-maligned economic reality: profit. Profit not only serves as a motive, but as a critical indicator for making economic decisions. Best of all, in the context of free trade, all sides always profit. Free trade makes for good neighbors, both locally and internationally. As Adam Smith put it, when goods and services cross borders, soldiers rarely do.

Discussion Questions

1. If all sides profit from any free trade, why do we tend to look down on "profit", at least those profits we deem to be excessive?

_____

_____

_____

_____

_____

2. Where did Marx miss the boat in promulgating his labor theory of value?

_____

_____

_____

_____

_____

3. How does Marxism fail to provide critical information to the marketplace? What is the inevitable result?

_____

_____

_____

_____

_____

4. How then does liberty lead to prosperity and tyranny to poverty?

_____

_____

_____

_____

_____

5. How does the subjective theory of value impact how we understand wages? How about minimum wage laws?

_____

_____

_____

_____

_____

6. How does free trade impact international relations?

_____

_____

_____

_____

_____

Memory Verses

I Corinthians 12:20-21, "But now indeed there are many members, yet one body. And the eye cannot say to the hand, 'I have no need of you'; nor again the head to the feet, 'I have no need of you.'"

Proverbs 27:7, "A satisfied soul loathes the honeycomb, but to a hungry soul every bitter thing is sweet."

Lesson 5
Money

Summary

The mutual profitability of free trade is grounded in some basic, but important economic laws and concepts—the Law of Marginal Utility, the Law of Comparative Advantage, and the Subjective Theory of Value. These may sound like complex and obtuse concepts, but they are nothing more than every day words that describe our every day activities. They describe what we already know and how we already live.

Understanding these basic principles in turn equips us to come to a basic understanding of the nature and function of money. Money's real value is rooted in how it encourages trade. And because all free trade creates profit for both sides, the more trading that happens, the more we all prosper.

Discussion Questions

1. What are some examples of barter in your own life? How satisfied were you with the arrangement?

_____

_____

_____

_____

_____

2. How does the Law of Marginal Utility explain why we would pay more for the first hamburger than we would for the tenth? How does this impact the value of trade?

_____

_____

_____

_____

_____

3. How does the Law of Comparative Advantage relate to the biblical notion of calling or vocation?

_____

_____

_____

_____

_____

4. Is the Subjective Theory of Value a form of philosophical relativism? How is it the same? How is it different?

_____

_____

_____

_____

_____

5. In what circumstances would a million dollars in cash be worthless? How about a thousand ounces of gold?

_____

_____

_____

_____

_____

6. Is money the root of all evil (I Timothy 6:10)?

_____

_____

_____

_____

Memory Verses

Proverbs 22:4, "By humility and the fear of the Lord are riches and honor and life."

Proverbs 21:5, "The plans of the diligent lead surely to plenty, but those of everyone who is hasty, surely to poverty."

Lesson 6
Inflation

Summary

Inflation has haunted countless nations and has even destroyed some. Too often, however, people confuse what inflation is with what it causes. Too many think inflation is rising prices, when instead it is an increase in the money supply, which will inevitably cause a rise in prices. We miss this in part because of the complex mechanisms of central banks that are sort of public and somewhat private that can create "money" out of thin air. Suddenly, "inflation" becomes a mysterious and unstoppable monster.

In the end, however, inflation is a moral issue, the result of governments consuming more than they produce, and thus dragging us all toward poverty. In this study, we will seek to take this complex tangle and make it small and clear. Economic principles, we would be wise to remember, do not change by changing scales. What is foolish for a boy selling lemonade on the street is foolish for massive countries. And what brings prosperity to your house is the same thing that brings prosperity to a nation.

Discussion Questions

1. Why do people still think that inflation is rising prices, or the result of a chain reaction of the greed of businessmen?

_____

_____

_____

_____

2. Why did so many goods and services used to cost so much less than they do today?

_____

_____

_____

_____

3. What is the locus of the greed that brings us inflation? Why is this first a political problem and only later an economic one?

_____

_____

_____

_____

4. If prices are simply the result of the division of goods and services by the money supply, what harm comes with an increase in the money supply?

_____

_____

_____

_____

_____

5. How does inflation relate to the biblical injunction against adding dross to silver, or against false weights and measures?

_____

_____

_____

_____

_____

6. Is inflation the result of economic ignorance or wickedness?

_____

_____

_____

_____

_____

Memory Verses

Proverbs 21:6, "Getting treasures by a lying tongue is the fleeting fantasy of those who seek death."

Isaiah 1:22, "Your silver has become dross, your wine mixed with water."

Lesson 7
Government

Summary

It is all too easy, after coming to understand how free markets work, to wish that we might have no government at all. Governments, after all, tend to get in the way of the economy. But, like liberty itself, the state, rightly understood, is a gracious gift from God. He gave us that state to protect us from aggressors foreign and domestic, against assaults on our persons and property.

In this lesson, we will endeavour to explain a proper appreciation and respect for government. Our goal is for students to understand the proper place and scope of the state and to identify what happens when states overstep their God-ordained bounds; to understand why the temptation exists for states to exceed their rightful role; and even to understand when and how we might wrongly ask the state to step beyond its boundaries.

Discussion Questions

1. What is the relationship between Adam Smith's notion of the invisible hand and the biblical understanding of the providence of God?

_____

_____

_____

_____

_____

2. What does the Bible say government exists for? Is it a necessary evil, or something else?

_____

_____

_____

_____

_____

3. What dangers come with giving an institution the "power of the sword" (Romans 13)?

_____

_____

_____

_____

_____

4. Is the sinfulness of man an argument for big government?

_____

_____

_____

_____

_____

5. What is the difference, morally speaking, between "legal plunder" and illegal plunder?

_____

_____

_____

_____

6. What is the most morally repugnant element of statism?

_____

_____

_____

_____

Memory Verses

Romans 13:1, "Let every soul be subject to the governing authorities. For there is no authority except from God, and the authorities that exist are appointed by God."

Proverbs 25:5, "Take away the wicked from before the king, and his throne will be established in righteousness."

Lesson 8
Debt

Summary

As Americans, we live in the most prosperous nation in the history of the world. But we live in a time of an increasingly hungry and intrusive government. Though a fallible document, the U.S. Constitution, like no other law before it, set the parameters of liberty that birthed our prosperity. Sadly, however, the Constitution has all but been forgotten by our federal government. It is honored in name only.

Given the accumulated debts of the federal government, we have all become debt slaves. Jesus, however, came, we are told, to set us free. He tells us that if we are believers, we are free indeed. In this study, we will consider the nature of our liberty, how the state endangers our liberty, and even how the church is often complicit in this treasonous affair.

Discussion Questions

1. What are some ways that the government is much more present in our day-to-day lives than it was one hundred years ago?

_____

_____

_____

_____

2. What is the importance of the Tenth Amendment to the U.S. Constitution? How relevant is it in our own day?

_____

_____

_____

_____

3. What does it mean to be free? Are we truly a free people?

_____

_____

_____

_____

4. What is the difference between the federal deficit and the federal debt? What are some of the results of government consuming more than it produces?

_____

_____

_____

_____

_____

5. What other ways has the Constitution been practically forgotten in our day?

_____

_____

_____

_____

_____

6. How is the church to blame for the growth of the size and scope of the state?

_____

_____

_____

_____

_____

Memory Verse

I Samuel 8:14-17, "And he will take the best of your fields, your vineyards, and your olive groves, and give them to his servants. He will take a tenth of your grain and your vintage and give it to his officers and servants. And he will take your male servants, your female servants, your finest young men, and your donkeys, and put them to his work. He will take a tenth of your sheep. And you will be his servants."

Lesson 9
Poverty

Summary

When it comes to economic issues, we can err by making decisions with our hearts and ignoring God's Word. Nothing exhibits these tendencies more than how we view "the poor." On the left, they cry out: "Something must be done." On the right some cry out: "Nothing must be done." In this lecture, we will endeavour to explain the correct understanding of what it actually means to be poor, as well as the varied causes of poverty. Some poverty is self inflicted; and some is not.

Having thought through the varying causes of poverty, we in turn must consider how best to help those struggling with poverty. The poor, Jesus told us, we would have with us always. He also told us, however, that when we give food to the least of these, we are giving food to Him. These then are not mere economic issues, but profoundly spiritual ones as well.

Discussion Questions

1. How many people in America are objectively poor? How many are declared to be poor by the state? Why the gap?

_____

_____

_____

_____

_____

2. Are all poor people poor because they are lazy? Are they poor because they are the victims of circumstance?

_____

_____

_____

_____

_____

3. What is wrong with treating all the poor the same?

_____

_____

_____

_____

_____

4. What did Jesus mean when He said, "The poor you will have with you always" (Matthew 26:11)?

_____

_____

----

5. Is "From each according to his ability; to each according to his need" a biblical concept?

----

6. What is the difference between equity and equality?

Memory Verses

Matthew 26:10-11, "But when Jesus was aware of it, He said to them, 'Why do you trouble the woman? For she has done a good work for Me. For you have the poor with you always, but Me you do not have always.'"

Proverbs 29:7, "The righteous considers the cause of the poor, but the wicked does not understand such knowledge."

Lesson 10
Equity

Summary

Can compassion come from the hands of the state? If not, what happens when the State tries to act as a compassionate benefactor? In contrast to this approach, God in His wisdom instituted an entirely different structure for dealing with the poor when He established Israel as a nation. What then can we can learn from God's wisdom concerning ministering to the poor?

One critical principle we will consider in this lesson is this: Caring for the poor must always be small scale and personal. It must be voluntary. And it must seek to make the poor come to prosperity, rather than remain mired in poverty. It must never enable foolish behavior, remembering that Scripture tells us that if a man does not work, neither let him eat.

Discussion Questions

1. Should the government play any role in providing for the poor?

_____

_____

_____

_____

_____

2. What are some ways that gleaning differs from government entitlement programs?

_____

_____

_____

_____

_____

3. How is welfare destructive to those who receive it?

_____

_____

_____

_____

_____

4. How ought we to understand the biblical command, "If anyone will not work, neither shall he eat" (II Thessalonians 3:10)?

_____

_____

_____

_____

_____

5. If God commands us to do something, does this mean the state should punish us if we fail to do so?

_____

_____

_____

_____

_____

6. How can the local church do a better job of caring for the deserving poor than the state?

_____

_____

_____

_____

_____

Memory Verses

II Thessalonians 3:10, "For even when we were with you, we commanded you this: If anyone will not work, neither shall he eat."

I Timothy 5:8, "But if anyone does not provide his for own, and especially those of his household, he has denied the faith and is worse than an unbeliever."

Lesson 11
Leviathan

Summary

The problem of an ever-growing and intrusive state isn't merely that it mucks up the economy. It is also a profoundly theological problem, as the state takes on itself the very attributes of God. Statism isn't just bad economics; it is idolatry. We find ourselves in dark waters precisely because we do not understand the proper limits of the state. We don't grasp the borders of sovereignty for the various spheres of authority that God has established.

In this lesson, we will again consider what we can learn about keeping appropriate limits on the state in view of how God established the nation of Israel. It is notable that God established executive rule, and a judicial system, but not a legislature. This fact provides a great deal of insight about the root of our troubles and the sufficiency of God's Word to govern us.

Discussion Questions

1. Should Christians who have a concern for the poor support government programs to meet the needs of the poor?

_____

_____

_____

_____

_____

2. What is sphere sovereignty, and why is it critical to understanding the calling and scope of the state?

_____

_____

_____

_____

_____

3. Should the state legislate morality? What else is there to legislate?

_____

_____

_____

_____

4. Why is education never the proper domain of the state? Why do so few Christians understand this?

_____

_____

_____

_____

_____

_____

5. Why did God not establish a legislative branch in constructing a government over His people in Israel?

_____

_____

_____

_____

6. What other governments has God established besides the civil government?

_____

_____

_____

_____

Memory Verses

Romans 13:4, "For he is God's minister to you for good. But if you do evil, be afraid; for he does not bear the sword in vain; for he is God's minister, an avenger to execute wrath on him who practices evil."

Ephesians 6:4, "And you, fathers, do no provoke your children to wrath, but bring them up in the nurture and admonition of the Lord."

Lesson 12
Outlook

Summary

Economics has long been known as "the dismal science." As we come to the end of our study, it is easy to understand why this perception exists. Put simply, sin wreaks havoc on the beauty of God's created order. This is why we find ourselves in such an economic mess. So then: Ought we to despair? Is there any reason that we might have hope about the future?

The answer is this: Our God reigns. Jesus told the disciples to be of good cheer, because He has already overcome the world. We would be of good cheer if we would remember that even the sinful, destructive behavior of a statist regime exists for His glory and our good. Our study began by affirming that God made, and therefore controls, everything. And nothing has changed. So be of good cheer.

Discussion Questions

1. Is this world destined to be utterly destroyed?

_____

_____

_____

_____

_____

2. How does our work relate to the work of Jesus as the second Adam bringing all things under subjection?

_____

_____

_____

_____

_____

3. In what ways does right now count forever?

_____

_____

_____

_____

4. Should we be optimistic or pessimistic about the long-term future?

_____

_____

_____

_____

_____

5. How does our obedience on earth relate to the coming of the new heavens and new earth?

_____

_____

_____

_____

6. What do you believe your role is in preparing for the great feast of the King?

_____

_____

_____

_____

Memory Verses

Genesis 3:15, "And I will put enmity between you and the woman, and between your seed and her Seed. He shall bruise your head, and you shall bruise His heel."

John 16:33, "These things I have spoken to you, that in Me you may have peace. In the world you will have tribulation; but be of good cheer, I have overcome the world."

Economic Terms to Master

Archimedes: The ancient Greek thinker who discovered the principle of the lever.

Arminianism: The theological school of thought named for Jacob Arminius which stands in opposition to Calvinism. Arminianism holds that unbelievers have some righteousness in themselves from which they can embrace the Gospel; that God's grace is able to be resisted by humans; that Jesus' death atoned for no one's sins, but made it possible for all people's sins to be forgiven; and that the elect are chosen on the basis of God's foreknowing who would choose Him and that believers can fall away from the faith.

Austrian School of Economics: School of economic thought committed both to free markets and sound money, such as a gold based system. See von Mises, Ludwig.

Barter: The act of trading goods for goods, minimizing the need for money. The difficulty in the barter system is finding an appropriate barter partner.

Budget Deficit: The gap between income and outgo in a given fiscal year.

Capital: Investment money used to start and sustain an economic enterprise.

Capitalist: The person who funds an economic enterprise. See Labor.

Chattel Slavery: Where the slave is considered the property of the owner.

Chicago School of Economics: The school of thought considered strongly pro-liberty, but not at all committed to a gold standard money system.
See Friedman, Milton.

Chilton, David: Author of *Productive Christians in an Age of Guilt Manipulators*, a book that was written specifically to answer the assertions made in Ronald Sider's book, *Rich Christians in an Age of Hunger*.

Coins: A holder of value which provides both a standard measurement of money combined with the authentication of said coin.

Debt Slavery: Slavery wherein the debtor becomes a slave to pay off a debt. When the debt is repaid, the slave is set free.

Dominion Mandate: The command of God to mankind, through Adam and Eve, to rule over all the earth and subdue it.

Economics: From the Greek, literally meaning "house law". The science of how limited resources are produced and distributed; or, how we create and receive our daily bread.

Federal Debt: The accumulated debt from annual budget deficits.

Federal Reserve: The central bank of the United States. It influences monetary and credit conditions in the economy and regulates banking institutions.

First Law of Prosperity: Consuming less than we produce leads to prosperity.

Free Market Economics: The belief that the exchange of goods and services in an economy without any outside influences is the best and most advantageous system to all people. It stands on the assumption that for any economic transaction to take place, both parties must necessarily be satisfied.

Friedman, Milton: The Nobel Prize-winning and highly influential twentieth-century economist associated with the Chicago School of Economics.

God's Institutions for Governing: The conscience, the family, the church, and the state. See Sphere Sovereignty.

Gold Standard: A money system whereby gold is directly or indirectly the medium of exchange.

Gresham's Law: Bad money drives out good money. For example, if you have a coin made of actual silver or gold, they will get hoarded (and removed from the active money supply) if the other coins in circulation are made of less valuable metals.

Hazlett, Henry: The author of *Economics in One Lesson*.

Industrial Revolution: That time period when many Western nations moved from a more agrarian economy, based on farming, to an industrial one, based on manufacturing.

Inflation: An increase in the money supply, the effect of which is to cause prices to rise. Inflation can occur naturally even when an economy is attached to a gold standard, but the vast majority of the time it is caused by governments. If a government wants to limit inflation—and this is a big if—then it simply has to monitor the price of gold: If gold prices rise, then there is too much available money (the money supply has been inflated); if gold prices drop, then there is not enough (we are suffering from deflation), and they need to expand the money supply.

Interstate Commerce: Commerce that crosses state lines.

Invisible Hand: The notion by economist Adam Smith of how free markets govern themselves to be of equal benefit to all participants. Some see this as the benevolent hand of God. See Smith, Adam.

Keynes, John Maynard: Author of the *General Theory of Money and Credit*. The man for whom the Keynesian School of economics is named.

Keynesian School: A centrist school of economic thought characterized by a commitment to inflating the money supply to promote spending, and therefore growth.

Labor Theory of Value: The theory that the value of a given good or service is equal to how much labor went into it. This notion is found in Karl Marx's *Communist Manifesto*.

Labor: The men who supply the work to build a good or provide a service. See Capital.

Laffer Curve: The notion that since tax rates influence productivity, two different rates will yield the same amount of income. A tax rate of 0% and 100% would yield $0 because in the former there would be no taxes, in the latter, no one would be willing to work. Presumably there would be similar ratios in between these figures, perhaps a 10% tax rate yielding the same as a 90% rate. Wise government then would choose the lower tax rate to yield the best return while costing the economy the least.

Law of Comparative Advantage: Nations and individuals should produce that for which they are at the greatest comparative advantage.

Law of Marginal Utility: Each additional unit of a given good or service is likely to be valued less than the one before. For example, a hungry man will value the first hamburger more than the second, the second more than the third, etc.

Law of Supply and Demand: If the demand for a particular good or service goes up and the supply stays the same, the price goes up. If the demand goes down, the price goes down.

Malthus, Thomas: Pastor and advocate of population control whose most influential theory was the warning that the growth in human population will always exceed man's ability to feed himself. See Simon, Julian.

Man's Material Welfare: The recipe for productivity, emphasizing the importance of tools. Man's Material Welfare equals Resources plus Labor times Tools. MMW=R+LxT

Manichaeism: The theological/philosophical view that holds there are two gods, equally powerful and co-eternal, one evil and the other good.

Market Value: The price that a consumer is willing to pay for a good or service.

Marx, Karl: Author of the *Communist Manifesto*, whose ideas helped launch the Communist revolution in Russia.

Mercantilism: An economic system that suppresses foreign trade through the use of tariffs and seeks to export goods and services while importing only money.

Money: A store of value defined by being a commodity that is useful, rare, durable, beautiful, portable, divisible, and universally valued. Gold is, historically, the commodity most commonly used as a store of value. Money is not wealth.

Objective Poverty: The reality when a person does not have enough calories to make it through the day, or lacks clothes or shelter.

Praxology: The study of human behavior. Key term in Ludwig Von Mises' *magnum opus, Human Action.*

Price Ceilings: No one may charge more than x for this good or service.

Price Controls: Price ceilings or price floors.

Price Elasticity: The measure of how much price changes influence demand.

Price Floors: No one may charge less than x for this good or service.

Price Level: The price of a good or service is not set by the producer but by the consumer.

Property Tax: A tax on real estate usually levied by a local government. This tax is especially onerous because it means that one may never truly own their property as they are in effect merely renting it from the government.

Reverse Elasticity: In rare circumstances, raising your price can increase demand.

Sider, Ronald: Evangelical scholar who embraces a more left-wing political position and who popularized this view in his book, *Rich Christians in an Age of Hunger.*

Simon, Julian: A professor who argued against the notion of a Malthusian catastrophe (that an increase in population has very negative economic consequences) and instead said that population is the solution to resource scarcities and environmental problems, since people and markets innovate. See Malthus, Thomas.

Skinner, B.F.: Psychologist who popularized the behaviorist school of thought which argues that man is a product of his environment.

Smith, Adam: Scottish economist and author of the highly influential book, *The Wealth of Nations,* considered to be the first modern work of economics and an advocate for free market economics.

Socialism: The economic system where the state controls the means of production, and all citizens are equally poor.

Sojourners: Evangelical left-wing group. See Wallis, Jim.

Sphere Sovereignty: God's institutions for governing must all remain within their own areas of influence. The conscience, the family, the church, and the government must do their own jobs and not interfere with the jobs of another institution.

Statism: The elevation of the state into the highest good.

Stewardship: God's injunction to man to tend the garden and take care of those things He has given us charge over.

Subjective Poverty: The perception that someone is poor because their financial abilities cannot match their desires.

Subjective Theory of Value: There is no objective value in a given good or service; it is dependant on what the consumer is willing to give in return.

Supply Side Economics: The school of thought that believes that economic growth can be most effectively created by lowering barriers for people to produce goods and services. Such barriers are taxes and regulations.

Surplus Capital/Profit: What we have left when we consume less than we produce.

Tariffs: A tax imposed by governments against trade goods offered from other countries. Creates artificially high prices for these goods and reduces demand for them.

Tax Freedom Day: That day when Americans stop working for the state and begin working for themselves. If, for instance, the total tax rate is 50%, tax freedom day would be July 1.

Tenth Amendment: The amendment to the Constitution of the United States that provides that powers not granted to the national government nor prohibited to the states by the Constitution are reserved to the states or the people. It was designed to restrain the growth and power of the federal government. See Tyranny.

Thirteenth Amendment: This amendment to the Constitution of the United States that officially abolished and continues to prohibit slavery and involuntary servitude, except as punishment for a crime.

Trade Deficits: Relating to the relationship between a nation's imports and exports. A negative balance of trade consists of importing more than is exported. See Trade Surplus.

Trade Surplus: A positive balance of trade consists of exporting more than is imported. See Trade Deficits.

Tyranny: Oppressive power exerted by governments.

Von Mises, Ludwig: Economist associated with the conservative Austrian School of Economics.

W.I.N.: Whip Inflation Now: A slogan from a marketing campaign of the Ford Administration. The absurdity of this is that the individual cannot in any way control inflation by his own actions. Inflation is controlled by keeping the money supply in a defined relationship with available goods and services. See Inflation.

Wage Controls: An artificially-imposed limit on what owners can pay laborers. It is seen as a way to control inflation. See Inflation.

Wallis, Jim: Head and founder of The Sojourners, an evangelical organization with left-wing political convictions.

Widget: A generic term used in economic discussions that stands for a produced good. Rather than coming up with a different product in each example studied, a person can just insert the word widget as in "the supply of widgets was growing faster than the demand."

Bibliography
Books for Further Study on Biblical Economics

From a More Biblical Perspective

The Coming Economic Earthquake Revised and Expanded by Larry Burkett

Poverty and Wealth by Ron Nash

A Biblical Economics Manifesto: Economics and the Christian Worldview by James P. Gills and Ron Nash

Baptized Inflation by Ian Hodge

Tithing and Dominion by R.J. Rushdoony

Economics: Principles and Policy from a Biblical Perspective by Tom Rose

From a Less Biblical Perspective

Economics in One Lesson by Henry Hazlitt

Basic Economics by Thomas Sowell

Economic Facts and Fallacies by Thomas Sowell

Whatever Happened to Penny Candy? by Richard Maybury

Economic Sophisms by Frédéric Bastiat

Advanced Reading

The Road to Serfdom by F.A. Hayek

Human Action by Ludwig von Mises

Man, Economy and State by Murray Rothbard

America's Great Depression by Murray Rothbard

Practical Money Management

Master Your Money by Ron Blue

Money and Marriage God's Way by Howard Dayton

Money Matters for Kids by Larry Burkett

The Total Money Makeover by Dave Ramsey

Biblical Economics Curriculum
QUIZ #1
(To Be Administered After Lecture 3)

1. What are the first four words in the Bible? _____
   _____

2. True or False? It is unspiritual to be concerned about issues of wealth. (circle one)

3. God has both sovereign power and sovereign _____.

4. True or False? Labor is a curse God placed on mankind after Adam's fall. (circle one)

5. Our bearing the image of God reflects not only our capacities (we think, and feel and will like God does) but our calling in exercising _____.

6. True or False? Non-Christians do not in any way participate in the dominion mandate. (circle one)

7. True or False? Man's work reflects the glory of God in creation. It is a form of re-creation. (circle one)

8. True or False? Economics is simple enough for even a child to understand. (circle one)

9. Man's Material Welfare = raw materials + labor ____ tools

10. The most basic key to prosperity is _____
    _____.

Biblical Economics Curriculum
QUIZ #2
(To Be Administered After Lecture 9)

1. True or False? Government is legalized force. (circle one)

2. Price floors forbid charging _____ than a standard set by law. Price ceilings forbid charging _____ than the standard set by law.

3. Who coined the term "invisible hand" to describe how providence directs free markets? _____

4. Francis Schaeffer said his greatest fear was _____?

5. Which amendment to the Constitution most restricts the size of the federal government? _____

6. _____ describes the gap between income and spending in a given year. _____ describes the accumulated gaps of the same over time.

7. _____ leads to prosperity. _____ leads to poverty.

8. List at least two different causes of poverty. _____
_____

9. True or False? Equity means receiving what is our due. (circle one)

10. True or False? The Bible says we should all enjoy the same level of prosperity. (circle one)

Biblical Economics Curriculum
MID-TERM EXAM

IDENTIFICATION: Give a brief description of the definition, and importance of each of the key terms or phrases below. 4 points each.

1. Dominion Mandate

_____

_____

_____

2. Law of Comparative Advantage

_____

_____

_____

3. Law of Marginal Utility

_____

_____

_____

4. Inflation

_____

_____

_____

_____

5. $MMW = RM + L \times T$

_____

_____

_____

6. Barter and Its Limits

_____

_____

_____

7. Subjective Theory of Value

_____

_____

_____

8. Stewardship

_____

_____

_____

9. Money

_____

_____

_____

_____

10. Profit

_____

_____

_____

_____

ESSAYS: Write an essay answering three of the five questions listed below. Be thorough, but be concise. 20 points each

1. Describe the impact a Darwinian view of creation versus a Biblical view will have on understanding economics.

2. Compare and contrast the subjective theory of value as it relates to labor with Marx's labor theory of value.

3. Describe how doubling the money supply of the Nation of Economic Illustration wreaks havoc on the economy of that nation.

4. Describe the posture the Bible calls us to have with respect to material wealth. Should we be concerned with these matters? Can we be too concerned with them? Use Biblical texts and examples. (You may, of course, use your open Bible.)

5. Explain how the Subjective Theory of Value encourages peace among neighbors and among nations. Include the impact of the Law of Comparative Advantage and the Law of Marginal Utility in your explanation.

Biblical Economics Curriculum
FINAL EXAM

IDENTIFICATION: Give a brief description of the definition and importance of each of the key terms or phrases below. 4 points each.

1. Legal Plunder

_____

_____

_____

_____

2. Government as Force

_____

_____

_____

_____

3. Tithe

_____

_____

_____

_____

4. Jubilee

_____

_____

_____

_____

5. Debt

_____

_____

_____

6. Ron Sider

_____

_____

_____

7. Poverty

_____

_____

_____

8. Liberation Theology

_____

_____

_____

9. Sovereignty of God

_____

_____

_____

_____

10. Government Licensing

_____

_____

_____

_____

ESSAYS: Write essays in answer to three of the five questions listed below. Be thorough, but be concise. 20 points each.

1. What is the difference between a rule of law and the rule of men? How does this impact the economic realm?

2. Discuss the rule of law, legal plunder and Romans 13. How can we best enjoy truly limited government?

3. Explain how both consuming less than we produce leads to prosperity and consuming more than we produce leads to poverty.

4. Discuss the difference between biblical care of the poor and how the state "cares" for the poor. Are governments able to be, and called to be, compassionate?

5. Why do some Christians end up supporting statist policies? What are some ways even Christian "conservatives" have supported the expansion of the size and scope of government.

Biblical Economics Curriculum
QUIZ #1 ANSWER KEY

1. In the beginning God.

2. False. God commands that we, like Him, be concerned with matters of wealth.

3. Authority.

4. False. Labor was a pre-Fall gift from God that only became cursed after the Fall.

5. Dominion over the creation, or simply dominion.

6. False. Even the labor of unbelievers is a fulfillment of the dominion mandate. Work is part and parcel of what it means to be human, to bear God's image.

7. True.

8. True, though economists and politicians often try to hide this fact.

9. X or Times. MMW= raw materials + labor X tools.

10. Consuming less than we produce.

Biblical Economics Curriculum
QUIZ #2 ANSWER KEY

1. True.

2. Less; more.

3. Adam Smith.

4. Statism.

5. 10th.

6. Deficit; Debt.

7. Liberty; tyranny.

8. Choice, calamity, laziness, oppression.

9. True.

10. False.